T0147039

DADDY'S
GIRL

DADDY'S GIRL

My Story of Surviving My Dad's Murder Trial,
Years of His Abuse, and My Life Now

RAINEY MAE

DADDY'S GIRL
MY STORY OF SURVIVING MY DAD'S MURDER
TRIAL, YEARS OF HIS ABUSE, AND MY LIFE NOW

iUniverse books may be ordered through booksellers or by contacting:

iUniverse
1663 Liberty Drive
Bloomington, IN 47403
www.iuniverse.com
1-800-Authors (1-800-288-4677)

*Because of the dynamic nature of the Internet, any web addresses or
links contained in this book may have changed since publication and
may no longer be valid. The views expressed in this work are solely those
of the author and do not necessarily reflect the views of the publisher,
and the publisher hereby disclaims any responsibility for them.*

*The views expressed in this work are solely those of the author
and do not necessarily reflect the views of the publisher, and the
publisher hereby disclaims any responsibility for them.*

*Any people depicted in stock imagery provided by Getty Images are
models, and such images are being used for illustrative purposes only.
Certain stock imagery © Getty Images.*

ISBN: 978-1-5320-7278-9 (sc)
ISBN: 978-1-5320-7277-2 (e)

Library of Congress Control Number: 2019904021

Print information available on the last page.

iUniverse rev. date: 04/05/2019

Contents

Finding out for the first time…

I came home from school one otherwise ordinary day, and was met on the front porch by my grandmother, my moms' mom. I could tell by her face that something was wrong, something devastating. I expected that I would hear my dad had taken his own life, as he had recently wrote several suicide notes. I was not prepared for hearing that he had taken someone else's.

Someone who's voice I just heard on the phone, recently talking to my mom. It was my dad's girlfriend's husband.

My parents were already, thankfully, divorced. After dating a stripper and some other country bumpkins…My dad met who he would kill for.

Apparently this woman and her husband had an open relationship. -But when she took it too far…throwing beer parties for underage teenage boys for instance, her husband wrote a personal ad, so perverted, it was meant to embarrass her, but my dad responded, and evidently she accepted.

I remember her convincingly, tearfully, lying to her kids when they asked her why she didn't have custody of them…she said, it was because their dad threatened to kill her if she sought custody. I didn't appreciate at the time, if that were true, -what mother would allow her children to be with such a dangerous person? I didn't know at the time, the truth of the matter, or appreciate her acting skills.

-Some background…

I grew up in rural, -small- town U.S.A

I soon found out how unforgiving that can be.

We were poor, but I was pretty much happily unaware of that…the only time I can remember I realized it, was when I really wanted a pretty, girly bathing suit, and what I got instead was a batgirl bathing suit that my grandmother found at the hotel she worked at as a housekeeper. That and not getting sprinkles on my ice cream, because they cost extra.

But, we had a lot of property, mostly woods, a pond, and a cow pasture. I think we mostly had them for pets, but I'm sure we had them for dinner as well.

My brother and I had oodles of forts, which were really just areas around a favorite tree that we raked free of every stone and weed, and claimed it as ours… we had a playhouse, that was a cleaned out chicken coop.

I took a lot of solace in these sweet, gentle animals. As well as our many dogs and other pets that would get dropped off at our house in the country, left abandoned by their owners. They like me, were abused by my father. He would kick them with his work boots, and they would run away, whimpering pitifully.

I would run after them… console them and coax them back home…

I understand now, that it is not unusual that despite this, there was a time that I was still close to my dad. In fact, the title of the book, is in part reference to a country song, that my dad used to play and sing. I listened to it in its entirety while writing this book, and it made me cringe. I think I pretended to like it as a child, to keep him happy.

This is just instinctive. I once caught him abusing a previous girlfriend's young daughter... I heard him scolding her, and when I walked into the bathroom to confront him, he was holding her up, shaking her violently above his head. The instant I walked in, with tears in her eyes, she started laughing, as he also pretended to be doing...

My dad had a quick temper, I learned quickly, at a young age, the difference between a flat head and Phillips head screwdriver, and various wrenches...when he wanted anything, he wanted it NOW.

He also had quite a sick sense of humor. I seem to recall him putting my hand in a vice grip in his workshop and being threatened "playfully" with a circular saw, going so far as to start it up...

This was just an average experience, I don't think I even told my mom about it...I told her some things, she would threaten him not to do it again, he would in turn threaten me, and his threats seemed a lot more credible...and this

would go on until they divorced when I was eleven.

He would drive so close the edge of our bank every time we went somewhere, and on our way home... that I would keep my hand on the door handle-just in case I would have to jump out of the truck, if we were to go over the edge.

My fear of heights is due to him, holding me out over a fence, and over a cliff in such a way that I could not grab a hold of anything to make myself feel remotely safe...I was completely at his mercy... this happened several times, in several locations...

He would crouch down on his hands and knees, and when I would walk back the long hallway of our mobile home to the bathroom, or to bed, he would jump out of the dark to scare me. I would try to walk as close to the wall, as far from the doorways as possible... but it didn't help.

He would stand outside looking in through

the kitchen window, so that when I would go out to the kitchen at night to get a bowl of cereal and sit at the table, he would grumble to get my attention, and there would be this crazed face starring in at me...demented...maybe I could see this being funny once...but when you do it repeatedly and you know it petrifies your child... it's sick.

He would hold me down, wrap my feet in a blanket so I couldn't move, and tickle me until I cried.

This is the kind of fear and torture that affects your whole life...I am extremely safety conscience, cannot stand to have my feet bound, and would you believe, suffer from anxiety...

Back to my dad's relationship

I'm not sure when their relations turned into a relationship, but as I mentioned, my mom had been communicating with his girlfriend's husband on the phone, trying to figure out what was going on, and if it was safe for any of the children to have their weekend visits.

Apparently my dads' girlfriend had been telling her husband she wanted to leave my dad, but he wouldn't let her…while she was at the same time telling my dad, that her husband was threatening to come take her back home, but she didn't want to go…

Thus the suicide notes. And thus the murder.

The Murder

My dad is a tall, intimidating man, and at the time, owned a lot of guns, he talked tough, but I don't think he was much without them. I don't know of him ever being in a fight in his life.

When her husband showed up with a truck full of friends, who I'm sure looked just as intimidating as my dad, to "rescue" her from my dad, who she claimed was holding her against her will, it ended in her husband's death.

He was shot six times, on the porch where I spent my childhood. The first two shots were fired from inside the trailer. Only my dad, his then girlfriend and her sister know who fired them. My dad then when out to the porch, and fired the

other four rounds, which were witnessed by the men who accompanied her husband.

While he was being arrested, his girlfriend told him to go to hell. -Soon after they were back together.

My dad got off on a temporary insanity plea with the help of a public defender, and only served ninety days in jail and some time in an outpatient mental health clinic.

I remember visiting him in jail, having to get patted down with a metal detector at fourteen, having to sit in the visiting room with him, alongside child molesters, and one of his cell mates who had threatened to rape me upon his release, I think just to jeer my dad, -asking my dad why he did this– and not getting a satisfying answer…I quoted this man's last words to him from the paper, as he plead for his life…demanding to know -how could he do this…

I remember seeing blood red letters on the newscast spelling out MURDER…and seeing a white sheet covering a body…trying to grasp that

is was my dad who did this, any good, childhood memories of this place, now a crime scene, tainted in an instant, and-forever…

I knew there should have been justice…but I remember being glad that he did not get the death penalty, I don't think I or my three younger brothers could have handled that.

Our punishment for his crime...

Along with the constant bombardment from the press, as this was sensational news, especially for the time, there was no escaping it, it was on the news, on the radio, in all the local papers. My mom and I decided to do an interview, and I asked the local paper, to the extent possible, to respect the fact that I lost my father that day too, to please give us some privacy...

I found notes, hand drawn pictures of the gun he used, left in my book bag at school, I remember trying to sit through a report on the murder, given by one of my classmates during my social studies class, as we would discuss current events, and apparently my teacher did not make

the connection to my last name… I finally ran out of the class…

The worst incident of this harassment, was when I found, what was wrapped up as a Christmas present, left on my mom's porch, addressed to our family…

I was so relieved to think that finally someone, was showing compassion to our family. I took it in to my mom, and she opened it in front of all her kids…we were excited to see what it was… and what at first looked like some kind of baked good, turned out to actually be horse manure, that someone took their time to wrap up and leave for us, just to be cruel.

Did they not realize that we didn't murder anyone? -That we felt just as bad about it…

There was even a drink named after him, the "joke" was six shots and you were dead… I patiently waited seven years, until I could walk into this hick bar, order that drink, tell them who I was, and walk out.

I couldn't even get a job as a dishwasher in town, because of my name…

After the trial…

After my dad served his time, I went with him to the trailer where the murder happened, to collect his things, unbeknownst to me at the time, so that he could move on with his life. I remember looking for bullet holes… still trying to accept what happened…

My dad and his girlfriend reunited and moved two and a half hours away…where no one knew their names or reputation. Where he had no problem getting a job.

They in part lived off the social security that she collected from her late husband. I'm told she spent what should have went to her children as well.

While he all but ignored his own biological children, they went on to raise her young son to call my dad, the man that murdered this boys' father, dad.

I only found out in recent years, they had told him that his dad died in a fire.

I was able to tell my stepbrothers' wife, the truth about what really happened to his dad. He had already been told some about it, from his uncle, his dad's brother. But I was able to verify it and fill in some details he did not have. This was awkward, sad, and satisfying to expose the truth, which he was owed.

When my stepbrother, her youngest of two children turned of age, and therefore the social security was depleted…His mom and my dad finally married, none of his children were invited to the wedding, not that I would have attended anyway, even if I had been. I just received pictures after the fact.

Lingering effects…

To say all of this, which occurred during my adolescence, -adversely affected my self- esteem, and my impression of society… would of course, be an understatement.

I –hated-whenever I would meet friends' parents for the first time for instance…and they would ask, who my parents were…what do they do for a living? -seemingly normal, but impossible questions… -How do you answer that?

Of course I rebelled. I became an alcoholic at age fourteen. Which led to years of other addictions, poor choices in relationships… sabotaging good relationships…and a host of problems… which took years to get over…or just

find peace with. The hardest of which has been to forgive myself.

I wore out the expression geographical cure… I travelled extensively, mostly up and down the east coast, but as far as Taiwan, and the Caribbean.

It has always been easier to be a stranger anywhere else than walk down the main street of my hometown.

Some of that travel may have just been my sense of adventure that I always seem to have had…I remember standing in my yard as a kid watching the jets fly over, wondering where they were going…occasionally trying to wave them down… to take me with them, wherever that happened to be…

But there is also the restlessness of trying to find a place that feels like home.

-Life now-

I don't wish to discuss much of my recovery process, only that it took years… and I cannot say enough good about AA. and Jehovah's Witnesses, their website is www.jw.org.

When I became a single mom, I actually returned home, to be closer to family. My mom had remarried, (and consequently re-divorced) and I am now the oldest of seven children. I'm not the only one with some permanent scars… but…for the most part, most of us, are doing well considering…

I went back to school, as a single mom with two babies, to become a Massage Therapist, something I had long wanted to do. I opened

and stayed in business for several years, right on the Main Street of downtown. Putting my small plaque, with my last name on my office, was quite a triumph for me.

I worked as a live in caregiver for several millionaires, because they hired me in spite of my dad's actions, or because they were totally unaware. –Because they hired me based on my character, my work ethic, my trustworthiness.

I worked as a nanny, drove school bus, managed a Bed & Breakfast, sold my artwork, as a self-taught artist in several of the states that I lived in, because I no longer allow other people to dictate to me, what my worth is, and what I can and cannot do.

I came so close to giving up, so many times, and I wouldn't have seen any of the places I traveled to, had the experiences, accomplishments, i.e. -now and author… or met my children…so PLEASE, if you're struggling...don't give up!

Their life-

If you met either my dad or his wife today, you would never expect a thing. As long as they can keep their routine…of shopping at Kmart and flea markets…washing their cars, and nothing infringes on that, they would appear like any of their neighbors. In fact, my dad can be jovial, friendly, he enjoys nature, he took us to movies, and fireworks…

But the reality is, my dad doesn't talk to his only brother, or most of his kids. In fact, my oldest brother named his daughter after my dads' mom. Our gram was one of the sweetest, brightest lights in my life. My dad has never seen this grandchild,

or my brothers' second child, and probably never will. My brother's feeling is "let sleeping dogs lie".

I did allow him to see my boys when they were younger, albeit supervised… but ever since I told my stepbrother the truth about what happened to his father; even though my dad and stepmom drive two and half hours in our direction to visit her mom. She doesn't allow him to visit us, even though we are only fifteen minutes away from her mom.

She has always called the shots, excuse the pun, and he's always allowed her to. Not to mention there is no monetary reason for them to visit us, like any inheritance that I suspect she is trying to secure from her mom.

Sadly, my stepmother has had some consequences. Her daughter committed suicide some years ago, in front of her own young children, which her daughter blamed in part, on never being able to come to grips with how her mother could marry the man that killed her

father. This books' title is therefore apropos for her too, as she evidently truly was her daddy's girl.

I reminded them recently…as they are getting older, that due to their lack of interest over the years, besides their other grievous sins, they will probably wish they had someone to help them out, but it wouldn't be either of their daughters.

Printed in the United States
By Bookmasters